The **Graham Kendrick**
Christmas Collection

The **Graham Kendrick**
Christmas Collection

We hope you enjoy *The Graham Kendrick Christmas Collection*. Further copies
are available from your local music shop or Christian bookshop.

In case of difficulty, please contact the publisher direct by writing to:

The Sales Department
WORLD WIDE WORSHIP
Buxhall
Stowmarket
Suffolk
IP14 3BW

Phone 01449 737978
Fax 01449 737834
E-mail www@kevinmayhewltd.com

Please ask for our complete catalogue of outstanding Church Music.

First published in Great Britain in 2000 by world wide worship.

© Copyright 2000 world wide worship.

ISBN 1 84003 631 1
ISMN M 57004 764 2
Catalogue No: 1450199

0 1 2 3 4 5 6 7 8 9

Cover design by Jonathan Stroulger

Music Editor and Setter: Rob Danter
Proof reader: Sally Gough

Important Copyright Information

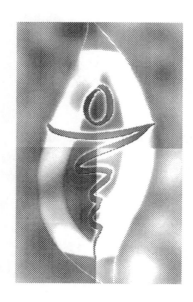

Contents

*Songs are listed alphabetically by first line. Where a song is also known by a title
this is indented and printed in italics.*

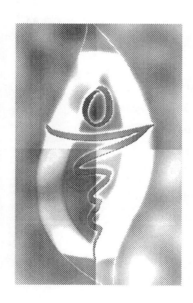

1 Ain't nothing like it

Words and Music: Graham Kendrick

1. Ain't no-thing like it, this joy I'm feel-ing. Ain't no-thing like it, what can I say? Ain't no-thing like it, my head is reel-ing.

To verse

Ain't no-thing like this hap-py day.

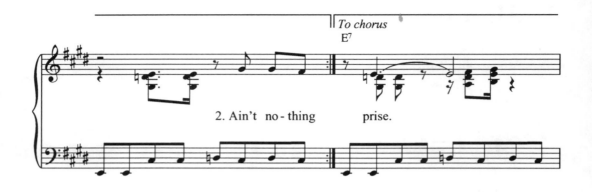

To chorus

2. Ain't no - thing prise.

Chorus 1

Seemed like an - gels

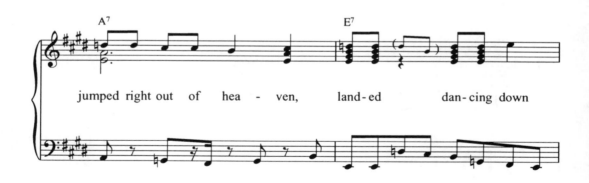

jumped right out of hea - ven, land - ed dan - cing down

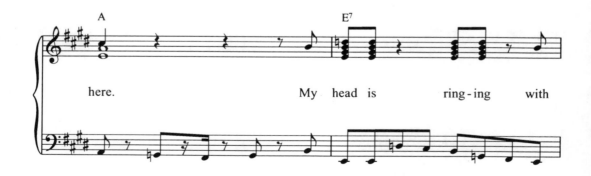

here. My head is ring - ing with

choirs of an - gels sing - ing. Ain't no-thing like this cra - zy

day.

2. Ain't nothing like it,
   this wild experience;
   could not believe my
   own ears and eyes.
   I thought I'd died and
   I'd gone to heaven.
   Ain't nothing like this big surprise.

3. Ain't nothing like it,
   the news they told us,
   for us a Saviour,
   a baby boy;
   born in a stable,
   the One we're looking for,
   he must be heaven's pride and joy.

Chorus 2   So excited,
           what a birthday party,
           Hallelujah O yeah!
           So delighted,
           we have been invited
           to celebrate
           his happy day.

RAP

Chorus 3   Glory, hallelujah,
           heaven's peace and joy be to you.
           Everything is alright now.
           Let's sing it, and shout it,
           tell the world about it.
           Ain't nothing like
           this happy feeling.

           Ain't nothing like this crazy day.
           Come on and join this happpy day.

2 Amazing grace!

Amazing grace - I was homeless

Words: v.1 John Newton; vs. 2, 3 Graham Kendrick
Music: American folk melody arr. Graham Kendrick

1. A - ma - zing grace! How sweet the sound that saved a

wretch like me. I once was lost, but

now am found; was blind, but now I see.

2. I was home - less, a stran - ger out in the cold,

ooh ooh ooh ooh ooh

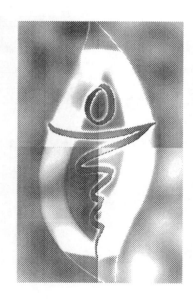

3 At this time of giving

The giving song

Words and Music: Graham Kendrick

Accelerating with each verse

At this time of gi - ving, glad - ly now we bring

gifts of good - ness and mer - cy from a heav'n - ly King.

1. Earth could not con - tain the trea - sures hea - ven holds for

you, per - fect joy and last - ing plea - sures,

love so strong and true. lai.

To continue

Last time

2. May his tender love surround you
   at this Christmastime;
   may you see his smiling face
   that in the darkness shines.

3. But the many gifts he gives
   are all poured out from one;
   come, receive the greatest gift,
   the gift of God's own Son.

Last two choruses and verses:
Lai, lai, lai . . . etc.

4 Be patient, be ready

White horse

Words and Music: Graham Kendrick

5 Can you believe it

Words and Music: Graham Kendrick

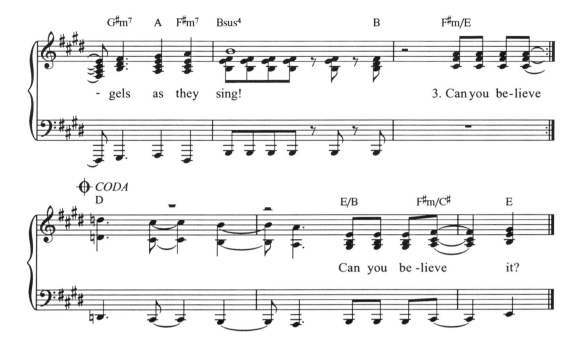

3. Can you believe it?
   His name shall be called Wonderful.
   Can you believe it?
   Counsellor, Mighty God.
   Can you believe it?
   Everlasting Father.
   Can you believe it?
   He is the Prince of Peace.

4. Can you believe it?
   This is good news, good news.
   Can you believe it?
   Don't be afraid!
   Can you believe it?
   The sun of Righteousness has dawned.
   Can you believe it?
   Joy to the world!
   Can you believe it?
   He came to seek, to save the lost.
   Can you believe it?
   Peace on earth!
   Can you believe it? (believe it),
   Oh, can you believe it?

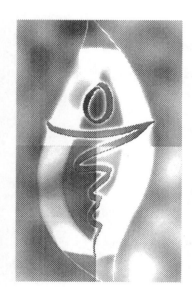

6 Can you see what we have made

Song for Christingle

Words and Music: Graham Kendrick

1. Can you see what we have made, for this ver-ry spe-cial day? An o-range for our pla-net home cir-cl-ing a-round the sun.
2. Count the sea-sons as we sing, sum-mer, au-tumn, win-ter, spring. Sing to God who sends the rain, mak-ing all things new a-gain.
5. There's a world I'm dream-ing of, where there's peace and joy and love. Light of Je-sus ev-'ry-where, this is my Christ-in-gle prayer.

7 Darkness like a shroud

Arise, shine!

Words and Music: Graham Kendrick

rise, shine, your light has come, Je-sus the Light of the

world has come. world, Je-sus the Light of the

world, Je-sus the Light of the world has come.

2. Children of the light, be clean and pure.
   Rise, you sleepers, Christ will shine on you.
   Take the Spirit's flashing two-edged sword
   and with the faith declare God's mighty word;
   stand up and in his strength be strong.

3. Here among us now Christ the Light
   kindles brighter flames in our trembling hearts.
   Living Word, our lamp, come guide our feet
   as we walk as one in light and peace till
   justice and truth shine like the sun.

4. Like a city bright so let us blaze;
   lights in every street turning night to day.
   And the darkness shall not overcome
   till the fullness of Christ's kingdom comes,
   dawning to God's eternal day.

8 Earth lies spellbound

Words and Music: Graham Kendrick

1. Earth lies spell-bound in dark-ness, sin's op-pres-sive night;
yet in Beth-le-hem hope is burn-ing bright.
Mys-ter-ies are un-fold-ing, but the on-ly sign
is a man-ger bed where a ba-by cries.

Chorus
Wake up, wake up, it's Christ-mas morn-ing,

2. Crowding stairways of starlight,
   choirs of angels sing:
   'Glory, glory to God
   in the highest heav'n.'
   Peace is stilling the violence,
   hope is rising high,
   God is watching us now
   through a baby's eyes.

3. Weakness shatters the pow'rful,
   meekness shames the proud,
   vain imaginings
   come tumbling down.
   Ancient mercies remembered,
   hungry satisfied,
   lowly, humble hearts
   are lifted high.

9 Father, never was love so near

Thanks be to God

Words and Music: Graham Kendrick

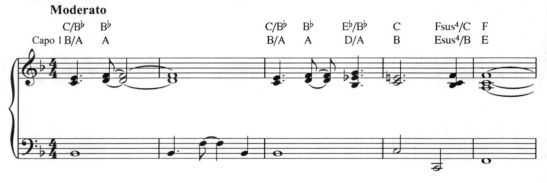

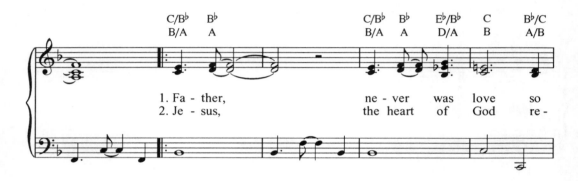

1. Fa - ther, ne - ver was love so
2. Je - sus, the heart of God re -

near; ten - der, my deep - est
vealed, with us, feel - ing the

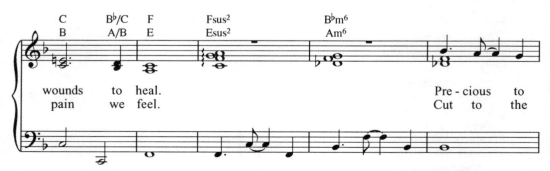

wounds to heal. Pre - cious to
pain we feel. Cut to the

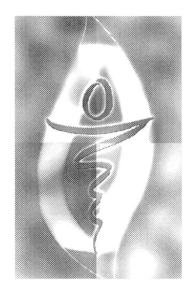

10 For God so loved the world

Words and Music: Graham Kendrick
Music arr. Christopher Norton

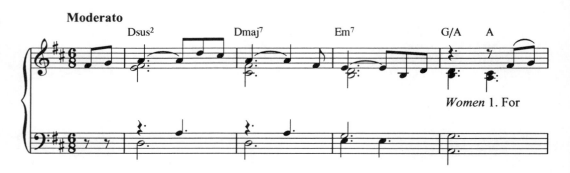

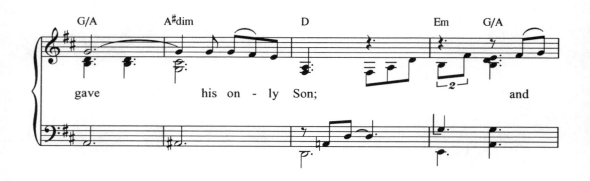

All
2. And God showed his love for you,
   when he gave his only Son;
   and you, if you trust in him,
   shall not die,
   but have eternal life;
   no, you shall not die,
   but have eternal life.

11 From heaven you came

The Servant King

Words and Music: Graham Kendrick

him, to bring our lives as a dai-ly of-fer-ing of wor-ship

To continue   *Last time*

to the Ser-vant King.   King.

2. There in the garden of tears,
   my heavy load he chose to bear;
   his heart with sorrow was torn.
   'Yet not my will but yours,' he said,

3. Come see his hands and his feet,
   the scars that speak of sacrifice,
   hands that flung stars into space,
   to cruel nails surrendered.

4. So let us learn how to serve,
   and in our lives enthrone him;
   each other's needs to prefer,
   for it is Christ we're serving.

12 Good news

Words and Music: Graham Kendrick

Brightly, with strength

1. Good news, good news to you we bring, al - le -

lu - ia! News of great joy that an - gels sing,

al - le - lu - ia! *Chorus* Ten-der mer - cy

he has shown us, joy to all the world;

for us God sends his on - ly Son,

al - le - lu - ia!

2. Let
3. Now

2. Let earth's dark shadows fly away,
   Alleluia!
   In Christ has dawned an endless day,
   Alleluia!

3. Now God with us on earth resides,
   Alleluia!
   And heaven's door is open wide,
   Alleluia!

13 Hear the sound of people singing
The Christmas Child

Words and Music: Graham Kendrick

1. Hear the sound of peo-ple sing-ing, all the bells are ring-ing for the Christ-mas Child.

In the streets the lights are glow-ing, but there is no know-ing of the Christ-mas Child.

Chorus

Oh, let this Child be born in your heart,

oh, let this Child be born in your heart, to -

2. Will our wars go on forever,
   and will peace be never
   at Christmastime?
   If we keep him in the manger
   then there is no danger
   from the Christmas Child.

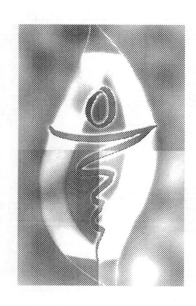

14 Heaven invites you to a party

Words and Music: Graham Kendrick

Joyful, with a strong rhythm

Hea-ven in-vites you to a par-ty, to ce-le-brate the birth of a Son; an - gels re-joic-ing in the star-light, sing-ing 'Christ your Sa-viour has come'. come'. (Leader) And it's for

star - light, sing - ing 'Christ your Sa - viour has

come'. And it's for you (and it's for you) and it's for
blast (let trum - pets blast), let mu - sic

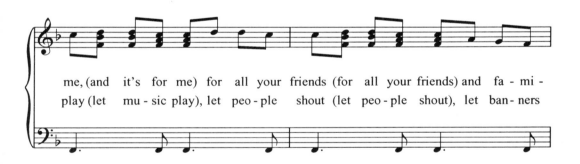

me, (and it's for me) for all your friends (for all your friends) and fa - mi -
play (let mu - sic play), let peo - ple shout (let peo - ple shout), let ban - ners

ly (and fa - mi - ly). Let trum - pets wave (let ban - ners wave).

15 He walked where I walk

God with us

Words and Music: Graham Kendrick

Quite quick, with a steady rhythm

(Leader)
1. He walked where I walk (he walked where I walk).
   He knows my frail - ty (he knows my frail '- ty),

(echo)

He stood where I stand (he stood where I stand). He felt what I feel
shared my hu - ma - ni - ty (shared my hu - ma - ni - ty), tempt - ed in ev - 'ry way

(Leader)   (All)

2. One of a hated race, (echo)
 stung by the prejudice, (echo)
 suff'ring injustice, (echo)
 yet he forgives. (echo)
 Wept for my wasted years, (echo)
 paid for my wickedness, (echo)
 he died in my place, (echo)
 that I might live. (echo)

16 High above the dark horizon

Morning star

Words: Graham Kendrick
Music: Graham Kendrick arr. Jonathan Savage

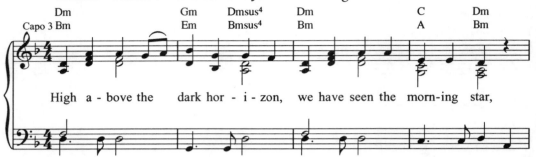

High a - bove the dark hor - i - zon, we have seen the morn-ing star,

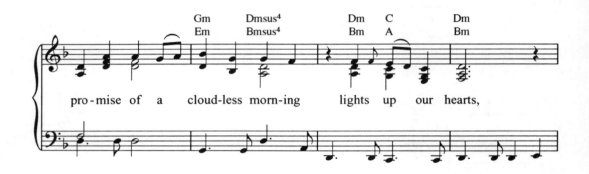

pro-mise of a cloud-less morn-ing lights up our hearts,

bright e - ter-nal day is break-ing, chas-ing sha-dows of the night,

o - pen fac-es up-ward gaz-ing, we a - wait the day of Christ.

2. Take the news to earth's far corners,
   soon the promised King will come,
   time's decay and death's dominion
   will soon be gone,
   there will be a new creation
   in the twinkling of an eye,
   hear his voice of invitation
   calling "Don't get left behind".

3. Coming soon on clouds descending
   East to West the skies will blaze,
   earth made bright with angel splendour,
   all the world amazed,
   every eye shall see his glory,
   King of kings and Lord of lords,
   saints from every age will greet him,
   caught up with him in the clouds.

4. So until that perfect morning
   we will run to win the race,
   till we're changed into his likeness,
   see him face to face,
   now unto the One who loves us,
   and redeemed us by his blood,
   be all honour, power and glory,
   so shall his kingdom come.

5. Now unto the One who loves us,
   and redeemed us by his blood,
   be all honour, power and glory,
   so shall his kingdom come,
   we have seen the morning star,
   we have seen the morning star,
   we have seen the morning star,
   we have seen the morning star.

17 Immanuel, God is with us

Words and Music: Graham Kendrick

2. He was despised and rejected,
   a man of sorrows acquainted with grief.
   From him we turned and hid our faces;
   he was despised, him we did not esteem.

3. But he was wounded for our transgressions,
   he was bruised for our iniquities.
   On him was the punishment that made us whole,
   and by his stripes we are healed.

4. He was oppressed, he was afflicted,
   and yet he opened not his mouth.
   Like a lamb that is led to the slaughter,
   like a sheep before his shearers he did not speak.

Suggested order: Chorus, v.1, v.2, chorus, v.3, v.4, chorus

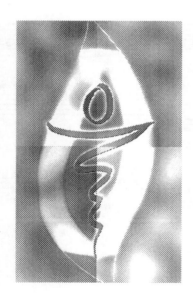

18 Immanuel, O Immanuel

Words and Music: Graham Kendrick

19 In the firelight
Beautiful night

Words and Music: Graham Kendrick

20 Joy to all the world

Anno Domini

Words: Graham Kendrick
Music: Graham Kendrick arr. Jonathan Savage

1. Joy to all the world, ring the free-dom bell, rise and wake the dawn of the new day.
2. Sound the trum-pet call, Christ is ri - sen, say to ev - 'ry - one your light is come.

Lift your voi - ces join

the chor - us. 3. Go through

all the earth, sing the new song, shout from East to West,

Here is your God.

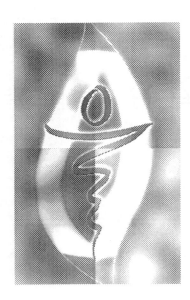

21 Let it be to me

Words and Music: Graham Kendrick

22 Like a candle flame

The candle song

Words and Music: Graham Kendrick

1. Like a can-dle flame, flick-'ring small in our dark-ness,

un-cre-a-ted light shines through in-fant eyes.

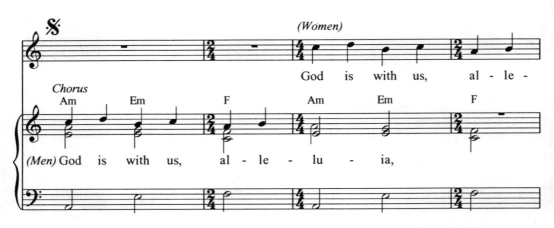

(Women) God is with us, al-le-

Chorus

(Men) God is with us, al-le-lu-ia,

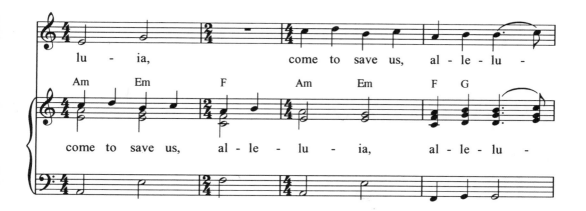

lu - ia,   come to save us, al - le - lu -

Am   Em   F   Am   Em   F   G

come to save us, al - le - lu - ia,   al - le - lu -

1, 2.   C   Dm⁷   G   *D.C.*   **3.** C   *D.S.*   *Last time* C

(All)
ia!   ia!   ia!

2. Stars and angels sing,
   yet the earth
   sleeps in shadows;
   can this tiny spark
   set a world on fire?

3. Yet his light shall shine
   from our lives,
   spirit blazing,
   as we touch the flame
   of his holy fire.

23 Look to the skies

Words and Music: Graham Kendrick

Triumphantly

1. Look to the skies, there's a cel-e-bra-tion, lift up your heads, join the an-gel song, for our Cre-a-tor be-comes our Sav-iour, as a ba-by born. An-gels a-mazed bow in a-do-ra-tion, glo-ry to God in the high-est heav'n, send the good news out to ev-'ry na-tion for our hope has

come. Wor - ship the King, come see his bright - ness.
Wor - ship the King, his won - ders tell. Je - sus our King is
born to - day, we wel-come you Em - man - u - el.

2. Wonderful Counsellor, Mighty God,
   Father for ever, the Prince of Peace.
   There'll be no end to your rule of justice,
   for it shall increase.
   Light of your face
   come to pierce our darkness,
   joy of your heart come to chase our gloom.
   Star of the morning, a new day dawning,
   make our hearts your home.

3. Quietly he came as a helpless baby,
   one day in power he will come again.
   Swift through the skies he will burst with splendour
   on the earth to reign.
   Jesus I bow
   at your manger lowly,
   now in my life let your will be done.
   Live in my flesh by your spirit holy
   till your kingdom comes.

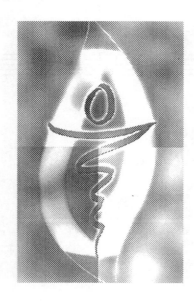

24 Make way, make way

Words and Music: Graham Kendrick

1. Make way, make way, for Christ the King in splen - dour ar-rives; fling wide the gates and wel-come him in - to your lives. *(Men)* Make

(Women) (make way,) (make way,) (for the King of kings;)
(Men) way, make way, for the King of kings; make

(make way,) (make way,)
way, make way, and let his king - dom in!

2. He comes the broken hearts to heal,
   the pris'ners to free;
   the deaf shall hear, the lame shall dance,
   the blind shall see.

3. And those who mourn with heavy hearts,
   who weep and sigh,
   with laughter, joy and royal crown
   he'll beautify.

4. We call you now to worship him
   as Lord of all,
   to have no other gods before him,
   their thrones must fall.

25 Meeknesss and majesty

This is your God

Words and Music: Graham Kendrick

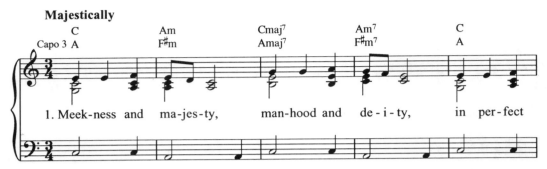

2. Father's pure radiance,
   perfect in innocence,
   yet learns obedience
   to death on a cross.
   Suffering to give us life,
   conquering through sacrifice,
   and as they crucify
   prays: 'Father forgive.'

3. Wisdom unsearchable,
   God the invisible,
   love indestructible
   in frailty appears.
   Lord of infinity,
   stooping so tenderly,
   lifts our humanity
   to the heights of his throne.

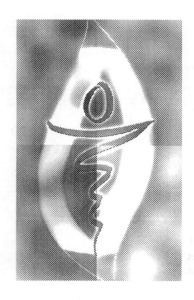

26 No room at the world

Words and Music: Graham Kendrick

With strength

1. I saw a pre-cious load on a lone-ly road when the sky was clear and cold, the don-key stum-bl'd, the young man held the reins. Well, the girl she look'd down and her face was white, she knew her time was near;

2. Well, the innkeeper laughed and his eyes were cold,
   the girl began to cry;
   that's just another way of saying: 'please.'
   So he threw down some straw on the cattle floor
   and chased the hens away,
   turned and slammed the stable door behind,
   shook his head in the starlight.

3. Well, it was late and cold in the garden grove
   when the soldiers came in view,
   and Judas smiled as they took him from behind.
   And the priest said: 'kill,' and the crowd went wild
   on their bloody holiday.
   They whipped him and they stripped him
   and they left him there on the cross to die.

27 Now dawns the sun of righteousness

Tell out, tell out the news

Words and Music: Graham Kendrick

Joyful and bright

1. Now dawns the sun of right-eous-ness, and the dark-ness shall ne-ver his bright-ness dim; true light that lights the hearts of men, on-ly Son of the Fa-ther, Je - sus Christ. Tell out, tell out the news, on ev-'ry street pro-claim a Child is born, a Son is giv'n, and Je - sus is his name! Tell

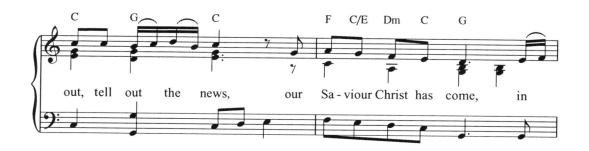

out, tell out the news, our Sa-viour Christ has come, in

ev-'ry tribe and na - tion let songs of praise be sung, let

songs of praise be sung!

2. Laughter and joy he will increase,
   all our burdens be lifted,
   oppression cease;
   the blood-stained battle-dress be burned,
   and the art of our warfare
   never more be learned.

3. So let us go, his witnesses,
   spreading news of his kingdom
   of righteousness,
   'til the whole world has heard the song,
   'til the harvest is gathered,
   then the end shall come.

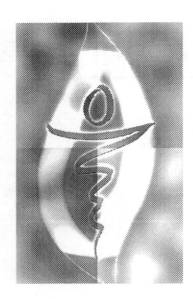

28 O come and join the dance

Words and Music: Graham Kendrick

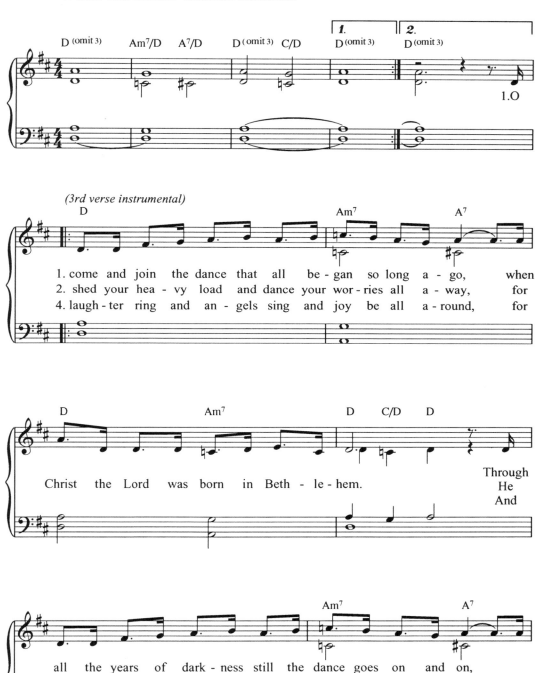

(3rd verse instrumental)

1. come and join the dance that all be - gan so long a - go, when
2. shed your hea - vy load and dance your wor - ries all a - way, for
4. laugh - ter ring and an - gels sing and joy be all a - round, for

Christ the Lord was born in Beth - le - hem.

Through
He
And

all the years of dark - ness still the dance goes on and on,
came to break the pow'r of sin and turn your night to day, O,
if you seek with all your heart he sure - ly can be found,

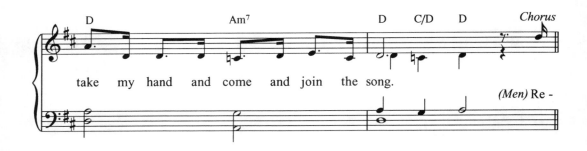

take my hand and come and join the song.

(Men) Re -

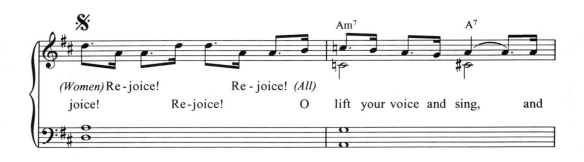

(Women) Re - joice! Re - joice! *(All)*

joice! Re - joice! O lift your voice and sing, and

o - pen up your heart to wel - come him.

(Men) Re -

(Women) Re - joice! Re - joice!

joice! Re - joice! *(All)* and wel - come now your King, for

1, 2, 3.

Christ the Lord was born in Beth - le - hem.

2. Come
3. *Instr*
4. Let

4. *D.S.* **5.**

hem. *(Men)* Re - hem. For Christ the Lord was born in Beth - le-

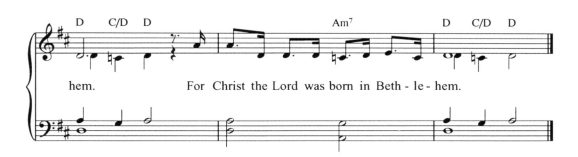

hem. For Christ the Lord was born in Beth - le - hem.

29 Once upon a universe

Words: Graham Kendrick
Music: Graham Kendrick arr. Jonathan Savage

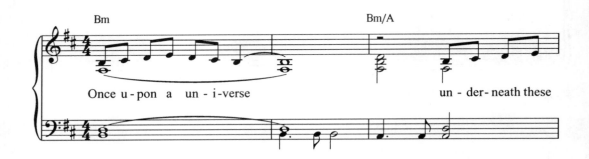

Once u-pon a un-i-verse un-der-neath these

same stars, the most a-maz-ing thing

hap-pened, the God who sent the ga-lax-ies cart-

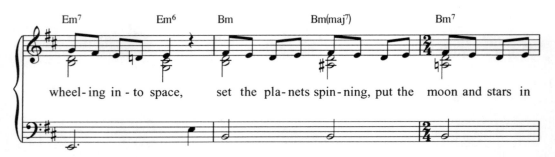

wheel-ing in-to space, set the pla-nets spin-ning, put the moon and stars in

30 O what a mystery I see

Words and Music: Graham Kendrick
Music arranged: Christopher Norton

Brightly

1. O what a mys-te-ry I see, what mar-vel-lous de-sign, that God should come as one of us, a Son in Da-vid's line. Flesh of our flesh, of wo-man born, our hu-man-ness he owns; and for a world of wick-ed-ness his guilt-less blood a-tones.

men'! 4. No

more then as a child of earth must I my life-time spend, his

his - to - ry, his des - ti - ny are mine to ap - pre - hend. O

what a Sav-iour, what a Lord, O Mas-ter, bro-ther, friend! What

mi - ra - cle has joined me to this life that ne - ver ends!

2. This perfect man, incarnate God,
   by selfless sacrifice
   destroyed our sinful history,
   all fallen Adam's curse.
   In him the curse to blessing turns,
   my barren spirit flowers,
   as over the shattered power of sin
   the cross of Jesus towers.

Women
3. By faith a child of his I stand,
   an heir of David's line,
   royal descendant by his blood
   destined by love's design.
   Men
   Fathers of faith, my fathers now!
   because in Christ I am,
   All
   and all God's promises in him
   to me are 'Yes, amen'!

31 Peace to you

Words and Music: Graham Kendrick

32 Rumours of angels

Words and Music: Graham Kendrick

1. Ru - mours of an - gels, vi - sions of light,
(2) an - gels, songs in the night,
3. Hearts full of long - ing, eyes filled with tears,

new star ap - pear - ing, pierc - ing the night.
deep in the dan - ger, un - quench - ab - le light.
na - tions are wait - ing, at the end of the years.

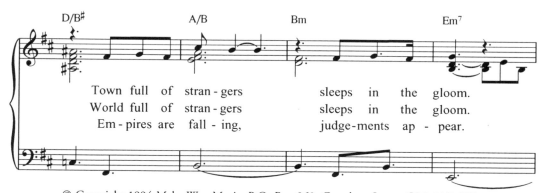

Town full of stran - gers sleeps in the gloom.
World full of stran - gers sleeps in the gloom.
Em - pires are fall - ing, judge - ments ap - pear.

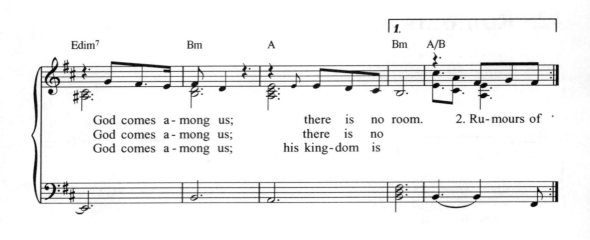

God comes a-mong us;   there is no room.   2. Ru-mours of
God comes a-mong us;   there is no
God comes a-mong us;   his king-dom is

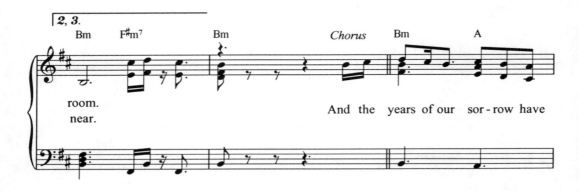

room.   And the years of our sor-row have
near.

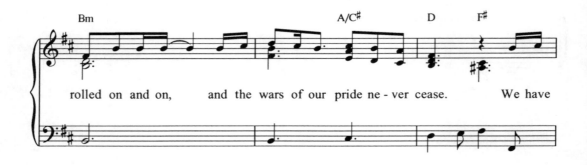

rolled on and on,   and the wars of our pride ne-ver cease.   We have

rav-aged the earth   with our   en-vy and greed,   tell me,

when will we wel-come his peace? When will we

wel-come his peace?

wel-come his peace? Oh, when will we wel-come the

Prince of Peace? Oh, Prince of Peace?

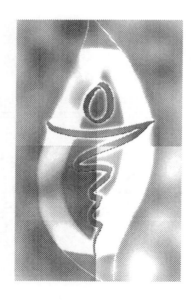

33 Since the day the angel came

Thorns in the straw

Words and Music: Graham Kendrick

1. Since the day the an-gel came it seemed that ev-'ry-thing had changed.

The on-ly cer-tain thing was the child that moved with-in on the

road that would not end, wind-ing down to Beth-le-hem,

so far a-way from home. 2. Just a

D.S. To finish

2. Just a blanket on the floor
   of a vacant cattle stall,
   but there the child was born.
   She held him in her arms
   and as she laid him down to sleep,
   she wondered, 'Will it always be
   so bitter and so sweet?'

   And did she see . . .

3. Then the words of ancient seers
   tumbled down the centuries:
   'A virgin shall conceive,
   God with us, Prince of Peace.
   Man of sorrows strangest name.'
   Oh Joseph there it comes again,
   so bitter, yet so sweet.

   And did she see . . .

4. And as she watched him through the years,
   her joy was mingled with her tears,
   and she'd feel it all again,
   the glory and the shame.
   And when the miracles began,
   she wondered, 'Who is this man,
   and where will this all end?'

5. 'Til, against a darkening sky,
   the son she loved was lifted high,
   and with his dying breath
   she heard him say, 'Father, forgive!'
   and to the criminal beside,
   'Today - with me, in Paradise.'
   So bitter, yet so sweet.

   And did she see . . .

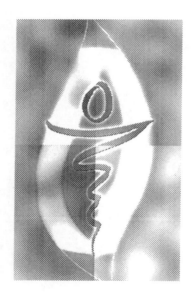

34 Sing, all the earth

Words and Music: Graham Kendrick

35 So many centuries

Nothing will ever be the same

Words and Music: Graham Kendrick

1. So ma-ny cen - tu-ries of watch-ing and wait - ing, but when the mo-ment came, well, no-bo-dy saw, tra-ders and tra-vel-lers hur - ried by, and life went on just like be - fore,

1, 3.

just like be-fore.

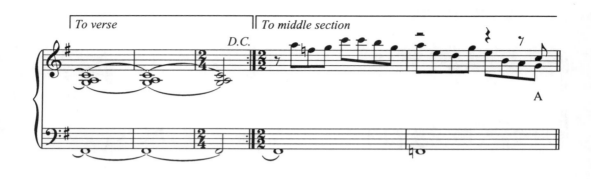

To verse   *To middle section*   D.C.

A

Bb   C

child   is born,   a Son   is giv'n,   and his

Bb   Bb/D   C/E   F   C   F/A

king - dom   of peace   will   ne - ver end.   A

Bb   C

child   is born,   a Son   is giv - 'n,   and his

king - dom of peace will ne - ver end, ne - ver end, no!

And

2. In all the clamour just a new baby crying,
   one more poor family shut out in the cold.
   Nothing unusual, sad to say,
   hasn't it always been this way?

   But nothing will . . .

3. So rare we recognise our history in the making,
   meet angels unawares and pass on our way,
   blind to the moment of destiny,
   while precious years just slip away,
   just slip away.

4. And now a door is standing open before you,
   casting its light into the darkness around;
   stop for a moment, step inside,
   tonight could be your Bethlehem.

   But nothing will . . .

36 Stars in our eyes

Seekers and dreamers

Words and Music: Graham Kendrick

1. Stars in our eyes, we're trav'l - ling moun - tains of stone

and such wild hope ri - ses in - side.

Day af - ter day, and moon - lit night

af - ter night, not know - ing where

you our trea - sures, lay at your feet the most pre - cious gifts that our hearts can bring, oh how we long to be there.

2. Weary and cold,
   sometimes we stumble and fall,
   and wonder why we carry on.
   But somehow this star
   has touched eternity deep
   inside our hearts, calling us near,
   leading us on.

3. When we set out,
   well we were searching for him,
   but something strange is happening;
   somehow it feels
   that he is searching for us,
   sending his star to guide us in,
   to lead us home.

Chorus B

We are the seekers, the dreamers,
mystical trav'llers, believers,
risking it all on a star,
knowing there's someone out there.
Searching the far constellations,
seeking the Source of creation;
love is the treasure we bring,
oh how we long to be there.

37 The King is among us

Words and Music: Graham Kendrick

2. He looks down upon us,
   delight in his face,
   enjoying his children's love,
   enthralled by our praise.

3. For each child is special,
   accepted and loved,
   a love gift from Jesus
   to his Father above.

4. And now he is giving
   his gifts to us all,
   for no one is worthless
   and each one is called.

5. The Spirit's anointing
   on all flesh comes down,
   and we shall be channels
   for works like his own.

6. We come now believing
   your promise of power,
   for we are your people
   and this is your hour.

7. *As verse 1*

38 This Child

Words and Music: Graham Kendrick

Calypso

1. This Child, se-cret-ly comes in the night, O this Child, hid-ing a hea - ven - ly light, O this Child, com- ing to us like a stran - ger, this hea - ven-ly Child. This Child, hea-ven come down now to be with us here, hea-ven-ly love

and mer - cy ap - pear,   soft-ly in awe   and won - der come
near   to this hea - ven-ly Child.
2. This
3. This   Child.   This Child.

2. This Child, rising on us like the sun,
   O this Child, given to light everyone,
   O this Child, guiding our feet on the pathway
   to peace on earth.

3. This Child, raising the humble and poor,
   O this Child, making the proud ones to fall;
   O this Child, filling the hungry with good things,
   this heavenly Child.

39 Tonight
Glory to God

Words and Music: Graham Kendrick

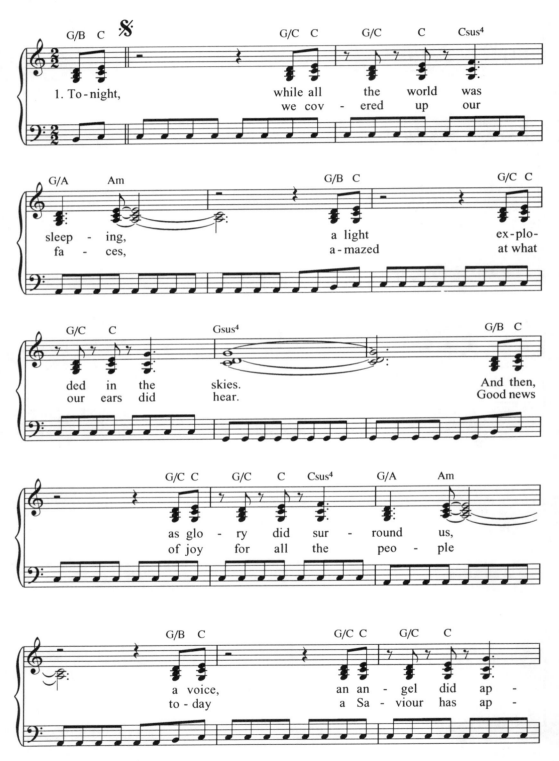

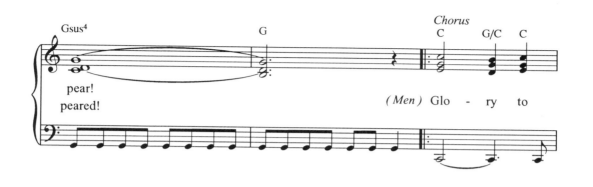

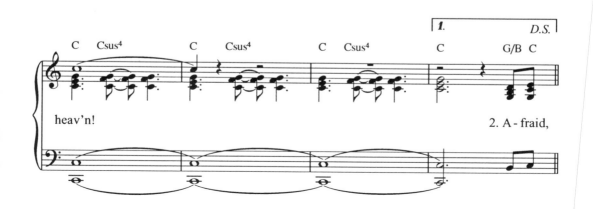

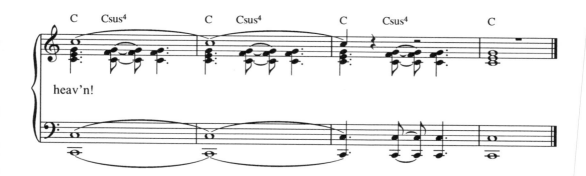

40 We will sing your song
You came from the highest

Words and Music: Graham Kendrick

We will sing your song, fol-low you for e-ver. We will be your hands reach-ing out a-gain. Your song goes on and on, your laugh-ter breaks the sil-ence. The sea-son of your joy will ne-ver, ne-ver end.

1. You came from the high-est, reached down to the low-est,

Peace to the peo-ple on earth.

G   D   Em   D   G

Peace to the peo-ple on earth.   Glo-ry to God in the high-est hea-ven.

Glo-ry to God in the high-est hea-ven.   Peace to the peo-ple on

Em   D/F♯   G   D   Em

Peace to the peo-ple on earth.

earth.

D.S. to vs. 2 and 3

Cmaj⁷   D   D   C   G/B   C   D

G   D   Am⁷   Em   D   D/C   Am

We will sing your song,   fol-low you for e-ver.   We will be your hands

reach - ing out a - gain. Your song goes on and on, your

laugh - ter breaks the sil - ence. The sea - son of your joy will

1. ne - ver, ne - ver end. And **2.** ne - ver, ne - ver end.

2. You came from the kindest,
   to suffer the cruellest,
   you are the message of love.
   You came from the purest,
   to die for the foulest,
   you are the message of love.
   Our God unrecognised,
   for ruined sinners crucified.

3. In the bustle of main street,
   the noise and the concrete,
   make us your message of love.
   In the turmoil of nations,
   or a heart's desperation,
   make us your message of love.
   Each step, each breath we take,
   yours is the love we celebrate.

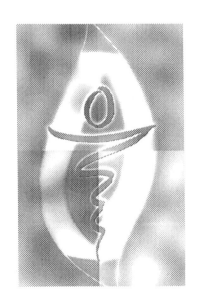

41 What kind of greatness

Words and Music: Graham Kendrick

O what else can I do but kneel and wor - ship you, and come just as I am, my whole life an of - fer - ing.

2. The One in whom we live and move
   in swaddling cloths lies bound.
   The voice that cried, 'Let there be light',
   asleep without a sound.
   The One who strode among the stars,
   and called each one by name,
   lies helpless in a mother's arms
   and must learn to walk again.

3. What greater love could he have shown
   to shamed humanity,
   yet human pride hates to believe
   in such deep humility.
   But nations now may see his grace
   and know that he is near,
   when his meek heart, his words, his works
   are incarnate in us here.

Also available:

The **Graham Kendrick** Christmas Collection CD

featuring the following selection of his worship songs from this book:

- *Earth lies spellbound*
- *Glory to God*
- *Good news/Sing all the earth*
- *Heaven invites you to a party*
- *Once upon a universe*
- *O come and join the dance*
- *Peace to you*
- *Song for Christingle*
- *Thanks be to God*
- *The candle song*
- *The giving song*
- *Thorns in the straw*
- *What kind of greatness*

Product code: 1490068